Frog's Eggs

Alex Ramsay and
Paul Humphrey

Illustrated by
Sarah Young

KU-260-875

Evans

4

6

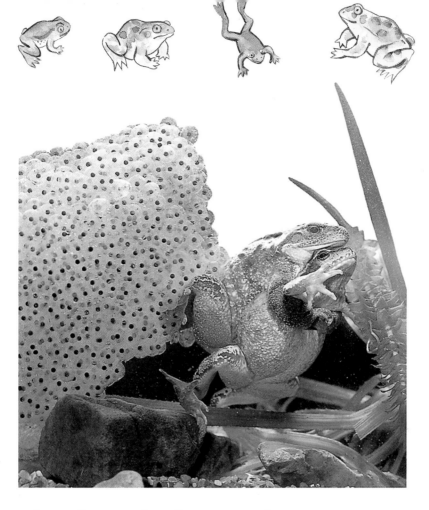

The female frog is laying
frog-spawn. The black bits in
the jelly are the eggs.

7

8

Yes, but we should take
some pond weed and pond
water, too.

We can put them in this old
fish tank.

10

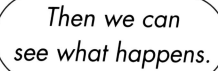

11

We've had the eggs for a
week now and look...

...they have started to hatch!

Those are the baby frogs.
They are called tadpoles.

14

They have very wiggly tails!

15

16

Now we can give them a
little piece of meat to eat.

21

…and their tails are getting shorter. Soon they will want to get out of the water.

23

We should put some rocks
into the tank so that they can
climb out of the water.

I'll put a
lid on, too!

24

25

They help them to swim fast.

Now we should put the frogs back into the pond.

29

How many stages of the frog
life cycle can you remember?

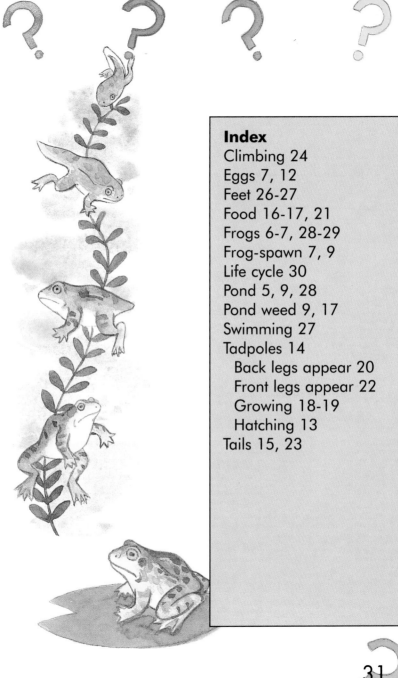

31